GREAT MOMENTS IN AMERICAN HISTORY

Victory at Sea

John Paul Jones and the Continental Navy

Scott Waldman

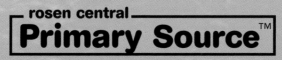

rosen central
Primary Source™

The Rosen Publishing Group, Inc., New York

Published in 2004 by The Rosen Publishing Group, Inc.
29 East 21st Street, New York, NY 10010

Editor: Eric Fein
Book Design: Daniel Hosek
Photo researcher: Rebecca Anguin-Cohen
Series photo researcher: Jeff Wendt

Photo Credits: Cover (left), title page, pp. 14, 30, 32 © North Wind Picture Archives; cover (right) illustration
© Debra Wainwright/The Rosen Publishing Group; pp. 6, 10, 29 © Hulton/Archive/Getty Images; p. 18
© Mary Evans Picture Library; p. 22 Réunion des Musées Nationaux/Art Resource, NY; p. 31 Scarborough
Borough Council, North Yorkshire, UK/Bridgeman Art Library

First Edition

Library of Congress Cataloging-in-Publication Data

Waldman, Scott P.
    Victory at sea : John Paul Jones and the Continental Navy / Scott
Waldman.—1st ed.
    p. cm. — (Great moments in American history)
    Summary: A biography of the American navy captain who served during the
Revolutionary War, focusing on his heroism in naval battles with the
better-equipped British fleet.
    ISBN 0-8239-4362-3 (lib. bdg.)
    I. Jones, John Paul, 1747–1792—Juvenile literature. 2. United
States—History—Revolution, 1775–1783—Naval operations—Juvenile
literature. 3. United States. Continental Navy—History—Juvenile
literature. 4. Admirals--United States—Biography—Juvenile literature.
[I. Jones, John Paul, 1747–1792. 2. Admirals. 3. United States.
Navy—Biography. 4. United States—History—Revolution, 1775–1783.] I.
Title. II. Series.

E207.J7W24 2004
973.3'5'092—dc21

                                                    2003002688

Manufactured in the United States of America

CONTENTS

Preface

‎❦‎

The American Revolutionary War lasted from 1775 to 1783. The war was fought between America and England. The war started because colonists in America no longer wanted to be ruled by the British. At the time of the war, England was one of the most powerful countries in the world. British leaders believed that the colonies in America were an important part of their country. They sent soldiers to America to stop the colonists from becoming independent. People in America fought against the soldiers. Soon the English and the colonists were at war.

As the war dragged on, many colonists became tired of the fighting. Some felt that the British would soon defeat them. Almost all of the war had been fought in America. However, one American

sea captain, John Paul Jones, wanted the British to feel what is was like to have a war fought in their homeland. Jones was a member of America's Continental navy. He had joined the Continental navy soon after it was created in 1775. In 1778, Jones brought the war to England. He was the captain of a ship named *Ranger*. He attacked the town of Whitehaven, England, on the coast of the Irish Sea. He tried to burn British ships in the harbor but was unable to. A short time later, however, he did capture a British ship called the *Drake*.

Most of the British fighting ships were better built than the American ships. Also, England had more money to pay more men to fight. They could buy better weapons, too. None of that scared Jones, though. He was willing to die to help the colonists win their independence....

John Paul Jones was born on July 6, 1747, in Scotland. He began his career as a sailor at the age of twelve. He also worked as a cabin boy on a ship that sailed to Virginia. Jones joined the colonies' Continental navy on December 7, 1775.

Chapter One

JOHN PAUL JONES GETS HIS SHIP

C aptain John Paul Jones stood on the deck of his ship as he sailed away from Lorient, France, toward England. It was early morning of August 14, 1779. The time had come for Jones to sail to England and take over any British ships he could. The sea air left his skin feeling sticky. The smell of fish filled his nose. Here on the open sea, Jones was happiest.

For a whole year, Jones had waited for a ship he could use to attack the English navy. He finally had one. Jones had just been put in charge of a ship, the *Bonhomme Richard*. The *Bonhomme Richard* was an old ship that had been turned into a war ship. Jones had made sure there were many cannons placed on the ship. He smiled as he looked at

the sea stretching out toward England in front of him. The *Bonhomme Richard* was sailing with four smaller ships. Together they were ready to meet any enemy. Jones stared at the rise and fall of the gray ocean waves.

"Captain!" Jones turned around to see who was calling him. "Captain! I've been looking everywhere for you." It was Richard Dale. Dale was the first lieutenant on the *Bonhomme Richard*. Captain Jones had ordered Dale to check in every hour on the hour. "The men are working very hard, sir. The ship is sailing along very quickly," Dale reported.

"Thank you, Dale. That will be all for now," said Jones.

Jones watched the men working on the deck of his ship. Some were raising the large sails. Some climbed up the mast to look for other ships. Others were getting the guns ready for battle. The sight of everyone working together made Jones happy.

Though Jones had been given the *Bonhomme Richard*, he had to find the men to sail it. He found many sailors in France. Many of them were from prisons. They came from many different countries. The men on the British ships, however, were all from England. Unlike Jones's crew, they spoke the same language. Jones knew it was important that all the men on his ship work together as a team during a battle. The *Bonhomme Richard* had forty large guns. A few men were needed to work each gun. If the men didn't work together as a team, the enemy would sink their ship. Jones only had a few weeks to get his men ready for battle. Could he do it?

Richard Pearson was a captain in the British navy. He was in charge of the *Serapis*.

A Fight on the High Seas

For the next month, Jones attacked many British ships. He captured them and took their crew as prisoners. His success stopped the flow of supplies to villages in England. People in the villages became worried. Yet, Jones wanted to do something that would scare the English even more. On September 23, 1779, while sailing off the coast of Yorkshire, England, he got his chance.

"Captain! Captain! There are many sails in the distance!" screamed the lookout sailor standing at the top of the mast. Jones ran over to the side of the boat and looked out over the sea. He could see some shapes that might be ships. "It looks like there might be over forty sails!" shouted the lookout.

One of the prisoners told Jones that it was a fleet of British ships. They were carrying supplies

for the British navy. "Then that's where we're going. Let's go get them!" ordered Jones. The crew moved the sails and got the guns ready for a big battle.

The fleet of British supply ships saw the *Bonhomme Richard* and turned away in another direction. However, two fighting ships that were sailing with the fleet turned toward the *Bonhomme Richard*. Before long, the *Bonhomme Richard* and the larger of the two British ships were sailing side by side. Though it was almost dark, Jones could read the name *Serapis* on the side of the British ship. *Serapis* had fifty guns, ten more than the *Bonhomme Richard*.

"What country are you sailing for?" called out the British captain, Richard Pearson.

Instead of answering the question, Jones raised an American flag. Both ships began shooting cannonballs at each other from a close distance.

BOOM! Smoke and the screams of men filled the air. Two of the *Bonhomme Richard*'s largest

guns had blown up. Many men were killed. There was a hole in the ship, too. Now, the other four large guns could not be used. Quickly, Jones came up with a plan. *Since the* Serapis *has more guns, there is only one way to win*, he thought. If the boats were tied together, the British could not use the large guns on their ship. Then the battle would have to be fought man to man.

"Sail close to them. We'll tie ourselves to their ship," ordered Jones. Jones tried a couple of times to get close enough to the *Serapis* to tie his ship to it. Each time he did, the *Serapis* easily got away. The cannonballs fired by the British continued to blast holes in the *Bonhomme Richard*. Captain Pearson cried out for Jones to give up.

"I have not yet begun to fight!" Jones shouted back.

The fighting between the sailors of the *Bonhomme Richard* and the *Serapis* lasted more than three hours.

Chapter Three

TWO SINKING SHIPS

A large gust of wind rammed the ships into each other. The ships got stuck together, front to back. Captain Jones had gotten lucky. It was the moment he was waiting for. He ordered his men to throw grappling hooks onto the British ship. Jones and some of his men tied ropes to the *Serapis*. The British sailors tried to cut the ropes. However, Jones's crew shot at them anytime they got close to the ropes.

With the ships tied together, the large guns were too close to fire on one another. Now, the battle would have to be fought hand to hand. Jones smiled. He'd win the battle—or die trying. A bullet flew closely past his head. Jones noticed that a few small fires had broken out on the *Bonhomme Richard*. Smoke poured out of the ship.

"Captain Jones! Come quick!" Jones raced over to the man who yelled for him. A fire had almost reached the gunpowder that was stored on the ship. If the gunpowder caught on fire, the entire ship would blow up! Jones and his men drew buckets of water from the sea. They threw the water on the flames. Finally, the fire died out.

Captain Pearson ordered his men to fire their cannons. *CRACK*! Pieces of wood flew into the air. A cannonball splashed into the sea. Since the ships were so close together, the cannonballs were blasting right through the *Bonhomme Richard*! The British cannonballs were tearing Jones's ship apart. Still, the crew aboard the *Bonhomme Richard* would not give up the fight.

"Captain! Captain! We need you below deck right now!" One of Jones's men was pointing down into the ship. Ocean water was pouring into it. British cannonballs had hit near the bottom of the *Bonhomme Richard*.

Men used pumps to get rid of the water as fast as they could.

"We're not going to give up now," said Jones. "Keep working those pumps."

"But, Captain, we'll sink if we don't give up to the British," said a nearby sailor. He looked tired and had blood all over his boots.

"I know it doesn't look good, but this is *our* fight," replied Jones.

"But Captain Jones! Our ship has been shot full of holes," said the tired sailor.

"I will not give up my ship. I'll fight for my country until they stop me. And that hasn't happened yet," said Jones as he quickly turned away.

John Paul Jones (in red jacket) is often called the "father of the U.S. Navy." Throughout his time in the navy, he was known for his bravery in battles and good leadership.

Chapter Four

THE BATTLE ENDS

"Captain, only three of our guns are still working. The British are hitting us with everything they've got. What should we do?" asked Lieutenant Dale.

Without answering, Jones hurried back to the deck of the *Bonhomme Richard*. For him, the battle was far from over and he had an idea. Grabbing a small cannon, he wheeled it to the edge of the ship. Instead of shooting at the British sailors, he shot at the main mast. This was the mast that held up much of the *Serapis*'s sails. If he could bring down the mast, the ship would be unable to sail. Jones fired at the mast many times. The mast took a lot of cannonball hits, yet it stood strong. Jones wondered how long he and his men could hold out.

Not far away, Richard Thompson and his family had heard loud noises while they were eating dinner. The Thompson family lived in Yorkshire, England. Thompson's wife and children had been holding on to him since the noises began. All were shaking with fear. The family and many others stood on the Yorkshire coast staring toward the sea. The coast was near Flamborough Head where the battle was taking place. The night sky was lit up with fires from the ships. By the light of the moon, Thompson could see that the ships had been tied together and that now the men were fighting by hand.

"Father, is the American captain going to take over our town?" asked Thompson's youngest son.

"No, son. Our navy is the best in the world. They'll sink his ship out there," replied Thompson. He wished he could believe his own words, though. Thompson hoped the American captain was not John Paul Jones. He

had heard stories about Jones and knew that Jones was the toughest captain on the sea. Even the best British captains would have trouble beating him.

Meanwhile, the men at the top of the *Bonhomme Richard*'s masts fired at the British sailors. Anytime a British sailor tried to fire one of the cannons on the deck of the *Serapis*, he was shot.

William Hamilton, a young American sailor, found a basket of grenades on the deck of the *Bonhomme Richard*. He crawled onto the British ship. The British sailors on the deck of the *Serapis* were too busy to notice Hamilton. Hamilton lit a grenade and dropped it into a hatch in the British ship. A large pile of weapons exploded. Many British sailors were killed. Hamilton's bravery had given the Americans a chance to win the battle. Could Captain Jones and crew finish off the *Serapis*?

The battle between the *Bonhomme Richard* and the *Serapis* left both ships badly damaged. About three hundred American sailors were killed in the battle. No one is sure of how many British sailors died during the fighting.

Chapter Five

A HERO TRIES TO SAVE HIS SHIP

Captain Pearson could barely see through all the smoke. However, he could see his enemy. Jones was still firing a gun at the main mast of the *Serapis*. Pearson had to stop Jones. If he didn't stop Jones, all would be over for those aboard the *Serapis*. Pearson gathered a group of men and ordered them to fight their way onto the *Bonhomme Richard*. The men grabbed their pistols and crept forward.

Jones figured out what Captain Pearson was planning. He ordered Dale to get his men ready for a hand-to-hand fight. The men gathered around Jones and hid behind barrels.

"Charge!" screamed Captain Pearson.

"Wait. Don't fire until I tell you to," whispered Jones. An angry group of British sailors ran

straight at Jones. He stared at them, not moving. "Now!" he screamed.

His men jumped up and fired at the British. Bullets flew everywhere. One hit the cannon Jones was firing and bounced off. Jones's men fired at the British from the masts of the *Bonhomme Richard*. The British sailors who were still alive ran back to their ship.

Jones once again fired his cannon. *BOOM!* The shot hit the middle of the main mast of the *Serapis*. The mast shook. Men on the decks of both ships froze. They could all hear the sound of the wooden mast cracking. Captain Pearson turned to face Jones. He knew he could fight no more. When the main mast broke, his ship would be lost. Jones had won.

Each captain ordered his men to stop fighting. After Captain Pearson gave up, Jones ordered him to be brought over to the *Bonhomme Richard*. Jones poured Pearson a glass of wine. Pearson had the blood of British

sailors on his uniform. Jones had the blood of his men on his uniform.

CRACK! Jones and Captain Pearson jumped. They turned toward the noise. The main mast of the *Serapis* finally broke apart. It hit the water with a large splash!

The British prisoners helped Jones's men fix the *Bonhomme Richard*. Water had been pouring into the bottom of the ship for hours. Parts of the *Bonhomme Richard* had been so ripped apart by cannonballs that it was possible to see through to the other side of the ship. For the rest of the night the men pumped water out of the sinking ship. They also fixed the mast of the *Serapis*.

By the next morning, the *Bonhomme Richard* was still low in the water. This was because of the flooding. Jones's men worked hard all day to fix it. They never had a chance to rest after the battle. Finally, Jones realized that the *Bonhomme Richard* was going to sink.

There was nothing he could do to stop it. He ordered all of his men and their prisoners onto the *Serapis*.

Jones wiped a tear from his eye as he said good-bye to the *Bonhomme Richard*. It had not been his ship for long, but it had served him well. First, the front of the ship vanished beneath the waves. Then, the rest of the ship stuck up in the air until it too sank under the waves. The ship disappeared forever. It carried with it the bodies of many men who had died fighting for their countries.

Jones knew that his victory would raise the spirits of the colonists back in America. He had just beaten one of the British navy's finest ships. His victory showed that the Americans were strong enough to stand up to the British. Jones was proud of himself and his men. They had just brought America—his country—one step closer to freedom.

GLOSSARY

cannonball (KAN-uhn-bawl) a heavy metal ball that can be fired out of a large gun

capture (KAP-chur) to take a person, an animal, or a place by force

colonists (KOL-uh-nists) people who live in a newly settled area

fleet (FLEET) a group of warships under one command

grappling hook (GRAP-uhl-ing HUK) a large iron hook, used to hold ships to each other

grenade (gruh-NADE) a small bomb that is thrown by hand or fired from a rifle

independence (in-di-PEN-duhnss) freedom

mast (MAST) a tall pole that stands on the deck of a ship and supports its sails

prisoners (PRIZ-uhn-urz) people who have been captured or are held by force

weapons (WEP-uhnz) something such as a sword, gun, knife, or bomb that can be used in a fight to attack or defend

Primary Sources

People learn about the past by studying many sources. Old works of art, letters, diaries, maps, and other things tell us about the people, places, and events of the past. The painting of Scarborough, England, on page 31, was done around the time of the famous battle between the *Bonhomme Richard* and the *Serapis*. People were able to see the battle from their houses in Scarborough. By analyzing the painting, we can try to imagine what life in Scarborough was like at that time.

Some primary sources we study are very unusual. The photograph on page 32 shows the remains of John Paul Jones after they had been buried in France for about 114 years. The photo helps us to construct and explain the story about Jones's remains being reburied in the United States in 1906. Sources such as the painting of Scarborough and the photo of Jones's remains help us answer questions about what happened in the past.

Richard Dale was born on November 6, 1756, in Virginia. Dale went to sea at the age of twelve. After the battle with the *Serapis*, Dale served with Jones on two other ships.

Sailors during the American Revolutionary War wore uniforms much different than U.S. sailors do today.

The battle between the *Bonhomme Richard* and the *Serapis* took place near the village of Scarborough, England. Many people from Scarborough were able to see the battle from the shore.

John Paul Jones died in Paris, France on July 18, 1792. He was buried in France. However, in 1906, Jones's remains (above) were removed from Paris and brought to the United States. He was reburied at the U.S. Naval Academy in Annapolis, Maryland.